The Ivory Gate

ALAN HALSEY's edition of the later version of Beddoes'
Death's Jest-Book was published by West House Books &
The Thomas Lovell Beddoes Society in 2003. His
articles on Beddoes have appeared in Beddoes Society
pamphlets, the *New Dictionary of National Biography*,
Agenda and *The Ashgate Research Companion to Thomas
Lovell Beddoes*. His recent collections of poetry are *Term
as in Aftermath* (Ahadada Books) and *Lives of the Poets*
(Five Seasons Press).

The Ivory Gate:
Later Poems & Fragments

Thomas Lovell Beddoes

edited by
Alan Halsey

RESCRIPT BOOKS

ReScript Books is an imprint of
Reality Street
63 All Saints Street, Hastings TN34 3BN
www.realitystreet.co.uk/rescript-books.php

The cover reproduces a detail from Beddoes' manuscripts

Printed & bound in Great Britain
by Lightning Source UK Ltd

First ReScript Books edition, 2011

A catalogue record for this book is available from the British Library

ISBN: 978-1-874400-50-9

Contents

Introduction..7

The Ivory Gate:
Surviving Fragments of Chapters I-VI...................15

The Ivory Gate:
Unplaced Songs & Fragments 31

Other Later Poems & Fragments.............................57

Notes 95

Index of Titles & First Lines...................................103

Introduction

1829 is commonly and reasonably regarded as the crux of Thomas
Lovell Beddoes' poetic career. Only a small part of his surviving
work, collected in the definitive edition by H.W. Donner, was writ-
ten after this date. The two volumes published in his lifetime – *The
Improvisatore* and *The Brides' Tragedy*, a highly-praised five-act play –
had appeared in 1821 and 1822, before his twentieth birthday. Dur-
ing the following two years he had written, and either abandoned
or partly destroyed, four more plays as well as occasional poems. In
1825 he left England and entered the University of Göttingen as a
student of physiology, surgery and chemistry; in the same year he
began writing *Death's Jest-Book*, describing it as 'a very Gothic-styled
tragedy'. A complete version of *Death's Jest-Book* was finished by
1829 and Beddoes looked forward to its imminent publication
when he sent it to London for the approval of his friends Bryan
Waller Procter ('Barry Cornwall'), Thomas Forbes Kelsall and
J.G.H. Bourne. But they – and particularly Procter – advised against
publication. It has been generally supposed that Beddoes set about
rewriting *Death's Jest-Book* in response to Procter's objections,
although the surviving revisions and additions tend to emphasise
and develop the elements which Procter found offensive. It seems
more likely that Procter merely triggered Beddoes' personal dissat-
isfaction with the work. The one fair copy of the later version con-
sisted of Act I only; along with more fragmentary passages it sug-
gests that while Beddoes' satirical bent had already undermined the
structure and scope of a five-act revenge tragedy he had struggled
and failed to find an alternative and sufficiently capacious form for

the excess his original conception continued to generate: the play of over-reaching constantly over-reaches itself. While this must remain an irresolvable point of interpretation it is apparent that much of Beddoes' relatively small body of writing in the last twenty years of his life (he committed suicide in 1849) consists of these revisions and additions. It is this aspect of his work which has been given particular prominence and it makes a seductive story: the most startlingly gifted third-generation English Romantic's cometary blaze gutters out as his vision of a 'triumph over Death' dissolves into a melancholy alcohol-fuelled obsession. There has been no collection solely devoted to Beddoes' later poetry which might offer an alternative account. All the poems gathered here can be found elsewhere, most notably in Donner's edition, but they have too often appeared as the scattered and outlying fragments of *Death's Jest-Book*'s ruins. I hope their publication in a single volume will offer a different and provocative perspective.

English Romantic poets shared the ambition to 'revive the drama'; only Beddoes devoted virtually all his mature writing to it. *Virtually* all – the exception, apart from occasional lyrics, was a work called *The Ivory Gate* which he announced in a letter to Thomas Forbes Kelsall dated 9 March 1837: 'I am preparing for the press, as the saying is, among other graver affairs, a volume of prosaic poetry and poetical prose. It will contain half a dozen Tales, comic, tragic, and dithyrambic, satirical and semi-moral: perhaps half a hundred lyrical Jews-harpings in various styles and humours [...].'[1] Writing to Kelsall again two months later he refers to 'the four chapters, containing as many tales, finished'.[2] In the same letter he transcribes the poem 'The New Cecilia', saying it is 'extracted from Chap V of the Ivory Gate – or lesser Dionysiacs – (my new book –)'. Of Chapter VI a single poem survives. It seems likely enough that Beddoes only 'finished' Chapters I-IV of the book which he said 'grows as slowly as a yew-tree', his one mature work of length cast in a form of his own devising. In 1838 he drafted a title page in which *The Ivory Gate* is subtitled 'DIDASKALIA—ELEUTHERIA—ANTHESTERIA / THANATOS

OR THE PRIVATE THEATRE / A STORY INCLUDING / DEATH'S JEST-BOOK' which perhaps summarises the work's themes rather than divisions by chapter. 'Eleutheria' was the feast of Liberty, 'Anthesteria' the Dionysian festival of flowers. Beddoes had told Kelsall he would include 'critical and cacochymical remarks on the European literature, in specie the hapless drama, of our day', which possibly accounts for the 'Didaskalia'. In what manner the 'story' would 'include' *Death's Jest-Book* is unclear and probably only implies that the two works were intended for the same volume, 'A dramatic Keepsake without engravings for 1838', a description suggesting that the draft may reflect no more than a fit of Beddoesian satire. There is no further mention of *The Ivory Gate* in his surviving letters and no evidence that he ever did offer it to 'the press'. But he retained sufficient interest in his 'lesser Dionysiacs' to carry the manuscript to England on his last visit in 1846, leaving it with Kelsall when he returned to Frankfurt in July 1847.

What became of *The Ivory Gate*? In his deathbed letter Beddoes asked Kelsall 'to look at my MSS – and print or not as *he* thinks fit.'[3] Kelsall devotedly carried out this request, editing *Death's Jest-Book* for publication in 1850 and the *Poems Posthumous and Collected* the following year. The second volume contained some poems from *The Ivory Gate*, presented as individual lyrics with titles supplied by the editor. In the longer term Kelsall hoped that Robert Browning would agree to edit a further selection of Beddoes' work and in November 1867 he sent Browning unpublished manuscripts including Chapters II and III 'from the "Ivory Gate", filling five closely packed sheets of letter paper.'[4] His own opinion of the tales was that they were 'crude & stiff & in the comic portions rather disagreeable'.[5] Browning concurred: 'external & skin-deep work'.[6] Since Browning had also concurred with Kelsall's suppression of 'disagreeable' passages in *Death's Jest-Book* – passages giving vent to Beddoes' best scurrilous humour – our curiosity is bound to be piqued and our regret at the loss of these tales can only deepen. For lost they were. At Kelsall's death Beddoes' papers were bequeathed to Browning, who kept them in an unopened tin box for ten years. By the time Browning and Edmund Gosse examined the contents Browning seems to have developed an aversion to Beddoes and passed on the editorial responsibilities to Gosse, whose edition of 1890 added ten poems and a dramatic scene to Kelsall's collection. Accounts differ as to the later history of the box of Beddoes' manuscripts, and to Gosse's part in it; the only certainty seems to be that it came into the possession of Browning's son Pip, after whose death in 1912 it could not be found. Fortunately James Dykes Campbell had been allowed to transcribe 'everything of importance' which Kelsall had not published, and his transcripts gave Donner the basis for his critical edition; but unfortunately Dykes Campbell did not consider the prose tales 'of importance' and only transcribed short fragments. It is curious that of Beddoes' immediate acquaintance only Procter, who had so objected to *Death's Jest-Book*, seems to have considered the tales worth preserving – but he had no say in the matter.

There is clearly an insufficient amount of extant material to allow anything amounting to a reconstruction of *The Ivory Gate*. Donner, the first and only previous editor to gather the fragments under the title, printed the chapter headings and epigraphs transcribed by Dykes Campbell separately, following these with the poems in 'an attractive arrangement'.[7] There seems little else an editor can do with most of the poems although I have altered Donner's arrangement so that poems which appeared on the same sheets or scraps of manuscript are printed alongside each other. I have also taken the more speculative course of including some poems under the chapter headings to which they probably belonged. This is not entirely conjectural. Kelsall's note published in *The Examiner* tells us that 'The Tale of the Lover' appeared in Chapter II; Dykes Campbell's brief list of contents strongly suggests that the Thanatos fragments belonged to Chapter I and some of the titles recorded in his transcript specifically place two other poems; we have it on Beddoes' own authority that 'The New Cecilia' appeared in Chapter V. The arrangement can do no more than hint at the tenor of the work; at times a reader might feel a faint yet palpable sense of what it once was. We at least have a cast of characters, ranging from the strictly mythological, who perhaps provided an overall framework, through the semi-mythical such as the maiden Thanatos and the Father of the Deep to others with such flesh-and-blood names as Edward, Ernest and Norman. Kelsall records that there was a love story, an intended marriage, a trial for murder, an execution: the territory will not surprise readers of *Death's Jest-Book* and yet the fragments suggest an altogether lighter treatment, a less determined field of wit. Death is never far from the author's thoughts, romantic love is subject to his sardonic humour, the dreams which enter through the Ivory Gate necessarily deceive – but while flowers, bees, birds and butterflies are as usual implicated in Beddoes' darkest symbolism they are also the vivid inhabitants of a sunnier world. In one fragment we seem to meet the author himself out walking in the Alps, cloud-watching and botanising. But who *is* the author? The 1838 title page identifies him as Theobald Vesselldoom, Beddoes' anagrammatic alter ego. Some poems are ascribed to 'T.V.'; we assume the rest are by 'T.L.B.' *The Ivory Gate* was quite possibly a heteronymic riddle.

The 'Other Later Poems & Fragments' inevitably form a less thematic collection. They are arranged here in roughly chronological order, many being datable by Beddoes' letters and other indications in the MSS. Even the songs, fragments and unused drafts of the later version of *Death's Jest-Book* will not seem to have any obvious coherence. Necessarily so: in his later years Beddoes would invent additional and dramatically irrelevant scenes in which to set new poems or add an extra embellishment by 'sticking in' another song; *Death's Jest-Book* becomes not so much a play as a cavernous treasure-house. He certainly seems to have felt that settings were required for many of his lyrics and this was probably the impetus for the poetry-and-prose format of *The Ivory Gate*. I have provided the settings wherever they are extant.

Readers familiar with the work will notice at once my omission of poem titles which appear in previous editions and anthologies. I have retained only those which (so far as I can establish) have Beddoes' authority. Many of the titles commonly given were supplied by Kelsall, who clearly felt that the poems should be made conformable to Victorian conventions which were nevertheless alien to Beddoes' cast of mind; a few were added by Gosse, a few more by Donner. The problem with these titles is that they are often highly determinative, either because they impose a flowery context such as 'Love-in-Idleness' or because they emphasise a specific aspect of a poem which Beddoes may not have intended, e.g. 'The Two Archers'. It is particularly acute where a poem lightly satirises the self-consciously poetic conventions to which the supplied titles belong: many of these poems are not exactly what they seem and a reader should be allowed to interpret them without unauthorised guidance. The problem extends to supplied titles which seem merely circumstantial or descriptive. Would Beddoes have entitled the unfinished poem beginning 'What silence drear', a furious blast at English official culture as relevant now as it was in 1844, 'Lines Written In Switzerland'? Probably not, particularly as the extant verses break off as their Shelleyan trajectory swerves to a scene set in the Caucasus – but, more to the point, we don't know, and an editor has no warrant to pretend otherwise. Similarly, would Beddoes have stepped so out of character as to give the quatrain beginning 'Poor bird', another transmutation of Shelley, the title 'On Himself'? Or bothered to favour the squib 'Drink Britannia …' with any title at all? In the latter two cases it has seemed a sounder course to preface the lines with the foregoing remarks in the letters which preserve them.

In other words I have tried in this collection to 'see Beddoes plain', to strip his later work (or what remains of it, surviving his own and others' penchant for destruction) of any paraphernalia not of his own making: to present the poems and fragments as they might have appeared in one of his notebooks. The result may seem stark; he may seem to be staunchly fulfilling Beckett's dictum 'Fail better'. But I hope there may be some advantage in seeing the work largely detached from the ravening demands of *Death's Jest-*

Book, the insatiable drive to 'make it cohere'. Can we regard Beddoes as not wholly consumed by his notorious death-fetish? When saying he was 'obsessed with death' we should at least acknowledge how often and cheerfully he mocks that obsession's absurdity; it may have been awareness of absurdity which chiefly possessed him, of life as much as death. Whatever it was it should not blind us to his metrical mastery, joy in the variety of verse and impish delight in transgressing its conventions. Anybody who reads these poems aloud will discover how inevitably word follows word, how precisely the lines are scored. Some are 'about' bright nothing, vagrant words which seem to have been effortlessly caught in mid-air: nonsense verse at its best, a riposte to an unmeaning world. The reader will find scatology and eschatology for specialists. A brooding sense of extinct species and the primeval earth is sounded more than once and yet 'Doomsday' is less a gloomy premonition than a glimpse of revolution too long deferred – Shelley's dead leaves driven by the west wind become not 'like' but literally the 'ghosts' who will 'quicken a new birth'. In 'Dream-Pedlary' and 'Far away' the glimpse is of personal loss; the note of isolation and despair in the last fragments may or may not be the expression of a dramatic or encrypted persona. The wonderfully calamitous syntax of a locution such as 'Wafted athwart downdashed' looks towards a poetics Hopkins would achieve many years later – the association is somewhat unexpected but perhaps Hopkins too felt 'utterly astray / Within the doubt-brakes of obscurest Thought'.

I must emphasise that I have only collected Beddoes' later work in English. During this period he also wrote prose and verse in German which will be found in Donner's edition with notes and translations. Much of the German writing arose out of his involvement in radical politics; his itinerant activity as public speaker and 'bearer of pamphlets' suggests a man with changed interests rather than a victim of daily hangovers. And although I have sought in this collection to detach the later writing in English from *Death's Jest-Book* I do not mean to suggest that any understanding of Beddoes' work can be attempted without reference to both earlier and later versions of that unique 'Dithyrambic in the florid Gothic style'.

Alan Halsey
Sheffield, June 2010

[1] *The Works of Thomas Lovell Beddoes*, ed. H.W. Donner (London: Oxford University Press, 1935), p.659.

[2] *The Works*, p.662.

[3] *The Works*, p.683.

[4] *The Browning Box: or, The Life and Works of Thomas Lovell Beddoes as reflected in letters by his friends and admirers*, ed. H.W. Donner (London: Oxford University Press, 1935), p.96.

[5] *The Browning Box*, p.100.

[6] *The Browning Box*, p.105.

[7] *The Works*, p.xxxviii.

The Ivory Gate:
Surviving Fragments of Chapters I-VI

Chapter I

The story of the first lover.

Forever to be continued.

Thanatos.

The father of the deep waiting for the end.

*   *   *

He: 'Shall I be your first love, lady, shall I be your first?
  Oh! then I'll fall before you down on my velvet knee
  And deeply bend my rosy head and press it upon thee,
And swear that there is nothing more for which my heart doth thirst,
    But a downy kiss and pink
    Between your lips' soft chink.'

She: 'Yes, you shall be my first love, boy, and you shall be my first,
  And I will raise you up again unto my bosom's fold;
  And when you kisses many one on lip and cheek have told,
I'll let you loose upon the grass, to leave me if you durst;
    And so we'll toy away
    The night besides the day.'

He: 'But let me be your second love, but let me be your second,
  For then I'll tap so gently, dear, upon your window pane,
  And creep between the curtains in, where never man has lain,
And never leave thy gentle side till the morning star hath beckoned,
    Within the silken lace
    Of thy young arms' embrace.'

She: 'Well thou shalt be my second love, yes, gentle boy, my second,
  And I will wait at eve for thee within my lonely bower,
  And yield unto thy kisses, like a bud to April's shower,

From moonset till the tower-clock the hour of dawn hath reckoned,
    And lock thee with my arms
    All silent up in charms.'

He: 'No, I will be thy third love, lady, aye I will be the third,
  And break upon thee, bathing, in woody place alone,
  And catch thee to my saddle and ride o'er stream and stone,
And press thee well, and kiss thee well, and never speak a word,
    'Till thou hast yielded up
    The margin of love's cup.'

She: 'Then thou shalt not be my first love, boy, nor my second, nor
    my third;
  If thou'rt the first, I'll laugh at thee and pierce thy flesh with
    thorns;
  If the second, from my chamber pelt with jeering laugh and
    scorns;
And if thou darest be the third, I'll draw my dirk unheard
    And cut thy heart in two, –
    And then die, weeping you.'

*   *   *

[Lament of Thanatos]

I was to wait, to wait my only time of youth away –
As many a maiden isle far in the sea
    From Adam to Columbus did for him
    Who was its destined finder –
Silent as a mountain before it falls, or as the world shall be on
    doomsday eve,
    Keeping the secret of to-morrow's morn,
    Still as a summer's noon –

*   *   *

18

Thanatos to Kenelm

[Dykes Campbell describes the setting as it appeared in Beddoes' lost story: 'This is sung by Thanatos, the wonderful beautiful maiden, who is Kenelm's companion in the woods of Madeira – hardly a mortal maiden – whom he found sitting by the old man described in 'The Father of the Deep'. The stanzas are thus introduced, the lovers walking in the primeval forests of Madeira':]

'I have no feeling for the monuments of human labour,' she would say, 'the wood and the desert are more peopled with my household gods than the city or the cultivated country. Even with the living animals and the prevailing vegetation of the forests in this hemisphere, I have little sympathy. I know not the meaning of a daisy, nor what nature has symbolized by the light bird and the butterfly. But the sight of a palm with its lofty stem and tuft of long grassy leaves, high in the blue air, or even such a branch as this' (breaking off a large fern leaf) 'awake in me a feeling, a sort of nostalgy and longing for ages long past. When my ancient sire used to sit with me under the old dragon tree or Dracaena, I was as happy as the ephemeral fly balanced on his wing in the sun, whose setting will be his death-warrant. But why do I speak to you so? You cannot understand me.' – And then she would sing whisperingly to herself:

> The mighty thoughts of an old world
> Fan, like a dragon's wing unfurled,
>   The surface of my yearnings deep;
> And solemn shadows then awake,
> Like the fish-lizard in the lake,
>   Troubling a planet's morning sleep.
>
> My waking is a Titan's dream,
> Where a strange sun, long set, doth beam
>   Through Montezuma's cypress bough:
> Through the fern wilderness forlorn
> Glisten the giant harts' great horn
>   And serpents vast with helmed brow.

The measureless from caverns rise
With steps of earthquake, thunderous cries,
   And graze upon the lofty wood;
The palmy grove, through which doth gleam
Such antediluvian ocean's stream,
   Haunts shadowy my domestic mood.

*   *   *

The Father of the Deep

   Who passed by sea or land
Beheld an ancient monumental man
Aye sitting by coeval ocean's side,
Titanic, upright, with large eyes whose use
Was but to weep to them invisible
And therefore twice dread woes. His watch no man
Had seen begun, nor yet hath seen him end.
Turned towards sunset, wishing for his own,
He there expects the coming of his son,
Eldest of things created save himself,
Over the western billow –

MS. Tragedy by T.V.

*   *   *

Epilogue to Chapter I

[Edward's Song]

I think of thee at daybreak still
   And then thou art my playmate small,
Beside our straw-roofed village rill
   Gathering cowslips tall,
And chasing oft the butterfly
   Which flutters past like treacherous life.

You smile at me and at you I,
  A husband boy and baby wife.

I think of thee at noon again,
  And thy meridian beauty high
Falls on my bosom like young rain
  Out of a summer sky:
And I reflect it in the tear
  Which 'neath thy picture drops forlorn,
And then my love is bright and clear
  And manlier than it was at morn.

I think of thee by evening's star,
  And softly, melancholy slow,
An eye doth glisten from afar,
  All full of lovely woe.
The air then sighingly doth part
  And, or from Death the cold or Love,
I hear the passing of a dart,
  But hope once more and look above.

I think of thee at black midnight,
  And woe and agony it is
To see thy cheek so deadly white,
  To hear thy grave-worm hiss.
But looking on thy lips is cheer,
  They closed in love, pronouncing love;
And then I tremble, not for fear,
  But in thy breath from heaven above.

CHAPTER II

THE LILY PLUCKED BY PROSERPINE

A Prose Tragedy

In the twilight silent smiled
All alone the daisy's eyelid,
Fringed with pink-tipped petals piled.
– In the morning 'twas no more;
In its place a gout of gore.
Break of day was break of heart,
Since, dear maiden, dead thou art.

Charonic Steps, a collection
of lyrics by T.V.

How could she be so beautiful and die,
I thought at first; yet we should rather think
How one so beautiful e'er came to life.

D's-J.B.

[The Tale of the Lover to his Mistress]

After the fall of Jupiter came Love one night to Psyche: it was dark in her cottage and she began to strike a light. 'Have done,' said he, in a low whispering tone – in which the hinge of some dreadful dark truth out of another world seemed to turn. 'Youth, power, and heaven have passed away from the gods: the curse of age has changed their shapes: – then seek not to look on me, Psyche; but if thou art faithful, kiss me, and we will then go into the darkness for ever.' – 'How art thou changed?' asked she; 'methinks you do but try me, jestingly, for thou canst only have grown more beautiful. That thou art more powerful I hear, for the night air is full of rushing arrows, and many are struck and sigh. Hast thou lost thy wings that were so glorious?' – 'Aye, but I am swifter than of old.' – 'Thy youth?' – 'Aye, but I am stronger: all must fall before me.' – 'Thy charms and wiles?' – 'Aye, but he whom I have once stricken, is mine for ever and ever.' – 'Why should I not see thee then? art thou Love no more?' – 'Aye; but not fleeting, earthly: eternal, heavenly Love.' – Just then the moon rose, and Psyche saw beside her a gaunt anatomy, through which the blue o' th' sky shone and the stars twinkled, gold promises beaming through Death, armed with arrows, bearing an hour-glass. He stepped with her to the sea-side, and they sank where Venus rose.

*   *   *

Epilogue to Human Woe by Kenelm

When we were girl and boy together,
　We tossed about the flowers
　And wreathed the blushing hours
Into a posy green and sweet.
　I sought the youngest, best,
　And never was at rest
Till I had laid them at thy fairy feet.
But the days of childhood they were fleet
　And the blooming sweet-briar breathed weather,
　When we were boy and girl together.

Then we were lad and lass together,
　And sought the kiss of night
　Before we felt aright,
Sitting and singing soft and sweet.
　The dearest thought of heart
　With thee 'twas joy to part,
And the greater half was thine, as meet.
Still my eyelid's dewy, my veins they beat
　At the starry summer-evening weather,
　When we were lad and lass together.

And we are man and wife together,
   Although thy breast, once bold
   With song, be closed and cold
Beneath flowers' roots and birds' light feet.
   Yet sit I by thy tomb
   And dissipate the gloom
With songs of loving faith and sorrow sweet.
And fate and darkling grave kind dreams do cheat,
   That, while fair life, young hope, despair and death are,
   We're boy and girl and lass and lad and man and wife together.

T.V. *fecit.*

CHAPTER III

[no surviving fragments identified]

Chapter IV

Witness (aloud): The Truth, the whole truth and nothing but the truth. (Aside:) I'll be damned if I speak a word of truth. (St Peter's cock crows again. Exit witness to Hell. Flourish of Penny Trumpets of Judgement &c. Curtain falls.)

Last scene in 'The Moral of it, or A Halfpennyworth of Rare Ben Jonson' by T.V.

> Old father longlegs would not say his prayers:
> Take him by the left leg and throw him downstairs.
>
> *Nursery Rhymes.*

> O Lie, O Lie, O Lovely lady Lie,
> Art thou indeed the daughter of the Devil?
> Then thou art greater than thy father, Lie,
> Ruling on earth under the name of Truth,
> While she is at the bottom of the well,
> Where Joseph left her.
>
> *D's J-B, Act 2.*

CHAPTER V

*   *   *

The New Cecilia

Whoever has heard of St Gingo
  must know that the Gipsy
  he married was tipsy
every night of her life with old Stingo:
and, after the death of St Gingo,
    the wonders he did do
    his infidel widow
denied with unladylike lingo –
'A parcel of nonsense together &
For St Gingo a fig, and a feather end.
    He no more can work wonder
    Than a clyster-pipe thunder
or I sing a psalm with my nether end.'

As she spoke it, her breakfast beginning on
  a tankard of homebrewed inviting ale,
Lo! the part she was sitting & sinning on
  struck the 100th psalm up like a nightingale.

Loud as birds in an Indian forest, or
A mystic memnonian marble in
The desart at daybreak, that chorister
  breathed forth its Æolian warbling:
& that creature seraphic & spherical
her fundament kept up its clerical
thanksgivings until she did aged die
  still cooing & praising alert in
  her petticoat swung like a curtain
let down on the tail of a tragedy.

Therefore, Ladies, repent & be sedulous
in praising your lords, lest, ah well a day!
a judgement befall the incredulous,
& their latter ends melt into melody.

*   *   *

CHAPTER LAST

HAPPILY MARRIED

THREE VOLUMES OF IT

By a fashionable author

*　　*　　*

Epilogue to Ernest's Story

Sung by NORMAN

Has no one seen my heart of you?
　My heart has run away;
And if you catch him, ladies, do
　Return him me, I pray.

On earth he is no more, I hear,
　Upon the land or sea;
For the women found the rogue so queer,
　They sent him back to me.

In heaven there is no purchaser
　For such strange ends and odds,
Says a jew who goes to Jupiter
　To buy and sell old gods.

So there's but one place more to search,
　That's not genteel to tell,
Where demonesses go to church:
　So Christians fair, farewell.

*　　*　　*

The Ivory Gate:
Unplaced Songs & Fragments

As I passed over the bridge I raised involuntarily my eyes and looked towards the perpendicular central rock of the Tödi towering above his mountainous brothers. At that moment a ray of the unseen sun broke through a slit in the cloudy mass in the sky and touched his snowy scalp. At another time I should have thought it more like inspiration descending on a hoary prophet, but now it reminded me of the last pale smile of my unknown fair. As I yet stood and looked, a song burst from the window of the hotel behind me:

O'er the snow, through the air, to the mountain,
  With the antelope, with the eagle, ho!
  With a bound, with a feathery row,
To the side of the icy fountain,
  Where the gentians blue-belled blow.
Where the storm-sprite, the raindrops counting,
  Cowers under the bright rainbow;
    Like a burst of midnight fire,
    Singing shoots my fleet desire,
    Winged with the wing of love,
    Earth below and stars above.

Let me rest on the snow, never pressed
  But by chamois light and by eagle fleet,
  And the hearts of the antelope beat
'Neath the light of the moony cresset,
  Where the wild cloud rests his feet,
And the scented airs caress it
  From the alpine orchis sweet:
    And about the Sandalp lone*
    Voices airy breathe a tone,
    Charming with the sense of love,
    Earth below and stars above.

Through the night, like a dragon from Pilate
  Out of murky cave, let us cloudy sail
  Over lake, over bowery vale,

As a chime of bells at twilight
   In the downy evening gale,
Passes swimming tremulously light;
   Till we reach yon rocky pale
      Of the mountain crowning all,
      Slumber there by waterfall,
      Lonely like a spectre's love,
      Earth beneath, and stars above.

The music of the Sandalp she sang of could not have come more startlingly to the brain of solitary shepherd than these sounds to me.

* Noted. See Hegetschweiler, p.44.

The Reason Why

I love thee and I love thee not,
I love thee, and I'd rather not,
All of thee, and I know not what.
  A flowery eye as tender,
  A swan-like neck as slender,
And on it a brown little spot
    For tears to fall afraid on
    And kisses to be paid on,
  Have other maidens too.
  Then why love I, love, none but you?
If I could find the reason why,
Methinks my love would quickly die.

Aye, knew I how to hate thee, maid,
I'd hate thee for I knew not what,
Excepting that I'd rather not
  Be thy friend or foeman;
  For thou'rt the only woman,
On whom to think my heart's afraid;
    For if I would abhor thee,
    The more must I long for thee.
  What others force me to,
  I turn me from; why not from you?
If I could find the reason why,
My disenchanted love would die.

But should'st thou cease my heart to move
To longings, that I'd rather not,
And tried I hate, I know not what
  My heart would do for mourning;
  Love I, – it bursts, love scorning.
O loveliest hate, most hateful love,
    This combat and endeavour
    Is what enslaves me ever.

I'll neither of the two,
    Or hate or love the love of you.
And now I've found the reason why,
I know my love can never die.

The Tree of Life

There is a mighty, magic tree,
That holds the round earth and the sea
In its branches like a net:
Its immortal trunk is set
Broader than the tide of night
With its star-tipped billows bright:
Human thought doth on it grow
Like the barren mistletoe
On an old oak's forehead-skin.
Ever while the planets spin
Their blue existence, that great plant
Shall nor bud nor blossom want;
Summer, winter, night and day,
It must still its harvest pay;
Ever while the night grows up
Along the wall of the wide sky,
And the thunder-bee sweeps by
On its brown wet wing, to dry
Every day-star's crystal cup
Of its yellow summer: – still
At the foot of heaven's hill
With fruit and blossom flush and rife,
Stays that tree of Human Life.

   Let us mark yon newest bloom
Heaving through the leafy gloom;
Now a pinkish bud it grows
Scentless, bloomless; slow unclose
Its outer pages to the sun,
Opened, but not yet begun.
Its first leaf is infancy,
Pencilled pale and tenderly,
Smooth its cheek and mild its eye:
Now it swells and curls its head –
Little infancy is shed.
Broader childhood is the next –

The Bells rang out suddenly with a merry peal; on one side was a newly opened grave for the devoted head of [one of] the two youthful maidens, on the other the open church door at which the clergyman was waiting to pronounce the happiest blessing of life on the wreathed brow of the other. ... So the jester of the Duke and the pet fool of the murdered Sebald were alone in the place. The former sate in the church porch playing with the wedding garlands, the latter with folded arms and vile melancholy under the ancient yew, half in the new-dug grave, and thus they sung:

SEBALD'S FOOL

Woe! woe! this is death's hour
Of spring; behold his flower!
Fair babe of life, to whom
Death and the dreamy tomb
Was nothing yesterday
  And now is all!
The maiden from her play
Beside her lover gay
  The churchyard voices call
    Tolling so slow,
      Woe! woe!

DUKE'S JESTER

Joy! joy! it is love's day;
Strew the young conqueror's way
With summer's glories young
O'er which the birds have sung,
Bright weeds from fairy rings;
  Here, there, away!
Joy, joy, the tree-bird sings,
Joy, joy, a hundred springs'
  Melodies ever say,
    Maiden and boy,
      Joy! joy!

THE FOOL

She cut the roses down
And wreathed her bridal crown.
Death, playful, culled her blossom
And tore her from life's bosom.
Fair maiden or fair ghost –
  Which is thy name? –
Come to the spectral host;
They pity thee the most
  And to the cold world's shame
    Soft cry they, low,
      Woe! woe!

At break of bright May morning,
   When triumphing o'er dark
   The sun's inspired lark,
All sprites and spectres scorning,
And laughing at all creatures' joys
Who could not hang and dive and poise
In their own web and flood of noise,
   Dropped out of his heart's treasure
    The sunbeam's path along
    Sparks and dews of song,
   As if there were no pleasure
    But to rise and sing and fly
    Winged and all soul into the sky:

   At break of this May morning
    A maiden young and coy
    Saw a wild archer boy
   Flying around and scorning,
Birdlike, a withered bowman's arts
Who aimed, as he, at roses' hearts.
Each cried 'Come buy our darts,
   They are with magic laden
    To deify the blood;
    An angel in the bud,
   Half-closed, is a maiden,
    Till opened by such wound she fly
    Winged and all soul into the sky.

   'You archers of May morning;'
    Said she, 'if I must choose,
    Such joy is to peruse
   In the star-light adorning
The urchin's eye, that my desire
Is for his darts, whose breath fans higher
The smitten roses like a fire.'
   So Love – 'twas he – shot smiling
    His shaft, then flew away;

Alas! that morn of May!
Love fled, there's no beguiling
　Repentance, but by hopes to fly
　Winged and all soul into the sky.

So one December morning,
　When the bold lark no more
　Rebuked the ghosts so sore,
When dews were not adorning
Aught but that maiden's cheek where wide
The blushes spread their leaves, to hide
The broken heart which such supplied;
　She sought the pair of May-day,
　And to the old one saith,
　'Let thy dart, stedfast Death,
Cure a forsaken lady;
　Its point is but for those who'd fly
　Winged and all soul into the sky.'

The Lily of the Valley

Where the hare-bells are ringing
　　Their peal of sunny flowers,
And a bird of merry soul
　　Sings away the birthday hours
　　Of the valley-lily low,
　　Opening dewily and slow
　　Petals dear to young and fair
　　For the prophecy they bear
　　　Of the coming roses –
The free bold bird of merry soul
Amidst his leaves cannot control
　　His triumphant love of spring.

Thou bird of joyous soul,
Why can'st thou not control
　　Thy triumphant love of spring?
I know that thou dost rally
　　Thy spirit proud to sing,
Because to-day is born
　　The lily of the valley.
Oh! rather should'st thou mourn;
　　For that flower so meek and low,
　　　Born with its own death-bell,
　　　Only cometh to foretell
　　　　Unpitying winter's doom,
　　Who in scorn doth lay it low
　　　In the tomb.

　　Vain is all its prayer:
It may flatter, as it will,
　　The ungentle hours
　　With its ring of toying flowers;
Unrelenting they must kill
　　With their scornful breath,

For the very petals fair
   Which the destined flower uncloses
      In its innocence,
      To plead for its defence,
By the prophecy they bear
  Of the coming roses,
      Sign the warrant for its death.

Dirge

Let dew the flowers fill;
   No need of fell despair,
   Though to the grave you bear
One still of soul – but now too still,
Since the still soul fled –
   One fair – but now too fair,
The lily being dead. –
For beneath your feet the mound,
And the waves that fleet around,
Have meaning in their grassy and their watery smiles;
And with a thousand sunny wiles
   Each says, as he reproves,
   Death's arrow oft is Love's.
Aye, doubt'st thou of the reading there,
   About all nature's movements seek:
Thou'lt find Death has his dimples every where,
   Love only on the lovely cheek.

'What do you think the mermaids of the Styx were singing as I watched them bathing the other day' –

> Proserpine may pull her flowers,
>   Wet with dew or wet with tears,
>   Red with anger, pale with fears;
> Is it any fault of ours,
> If Pluto be an amorous king
>   And come home nightly, laden
> Underneath his broad bat-wing
>   With a gentle earthly maiden?
> Is it so, Wind, is it so?
> All that I and you do know
> Is that we saw fly and fix
> 'Mongst the flowers and reeds of Styx,
>   Yesterday,
> Where the Furies made their hay
> For a bed of tiger cubs,
> A great fly of Beelzebub's,
> The bee of hearts, which mortals name
> Cupid, Love, and Fie for shame.
>
> Proserpine may weep in rage,
>   But ere I and you have done
>   Kissing, bathing in the sun,
> What I have in yonder cage,
>   She shall guess and ask in vain,
> Bird or serpent, wild or tame;
>   But if Pluto does 't again,
> It shall sing out loud his shame.
>   What hast caught then? What hast caught?
> Nothing but a poet's thought,
>   Which so light did fall and fix
> · 'Mongst the flowers and reeds of Styx,
>   Yesterday,
> Where the Furies made their hay
> For a bed of tiger cubs,

A great fly of Beelzebub's,
The bee of hearts, which mortals name
Cupid, Love, and Fie for shame.

As veined petal closes over
  A dewy spark
  Ere Eve is dark,
And starry fireflies flit and hover,
  Dreams of the Rose
  O'er it repose;
So bend thy head, and sleep awhile
In the Moon's visionary smile.

And in that rosy rosy hour
When bird sung out and scented flower
Came words to me from heaven above:
'Awake, young heart, awake and love.'

T.V.

The Flowery Alchymist

Hist, oh hist!
My pretty pale young violet,
    Thy moony cheek uncover;
Lift that hood of fallen sky,
    And my lips once more I'll wet
Against the dew-ball of thine eye.
                Hist, oh hist!

So a leafy whisper said
Underneath a sweet-briar shade.
    Guess the lady-blossom's lover!
'Twas the flowery Alchymist,
    A stinging gay intriguing fellow,
    The wildest bee in black and yellow.

Hist, oh hist!
My pretty pale young violet!
    Glowworm's lightning blind me
When I leave my bud's embrace,
    When I traitorously forget
Thy cerulean baby's grace.
                Hist, oh hist!

The very next night he told the tale
To a little lily of the vale,
    And the poor young violet died of shame.
Oh! fie, thou flowery Alchymist,
    Thou stinging, gay, intriguing fellow,
    Thou wildest bee in black and yellow!

Flowed many a woodbird's voice, and insects played
On wings of diamond o'er the murmuring tide,
So on the billows of thy ocean's heaven,
Dark with the azure weight of midnight hours,
Thy marble shadow like a root of towers
Young city of the sea, –

Silenus in Proteus

Oh those were happy days, heaped up with wine-skins,
And ivy-wreathed and thyrsus-swinging days,
Swimming like streamy-tressed wanton Bacchantes,
When I was with thee and sat kingly on thee,
My ass of asses. Then quite full of wine –
Morning, eve – and leaning on a fawn,
Still pretty steady, and on t'other side
Some vinous-lipped nymph of Ariadne,
Her bosom a soft cushion for my right:
Half dreaming and half waking, both in bliss,
I sat upon my ass and laughed at Jove.
But thou art dead, my dapple, and I too
Shall ride thee soon about the Elysian meadow,
Almost a skeleton as well as thou.
And why, oh dearest, could'st not keep thy legs
That sacred pair, sacred to sacred me?
Was this thy gratitude for pats and fondlings,
To die like any other mortal ass?
Was it for this, oh son of Semele,
I taught thee then, a little tumbling one,
To suck the goatskin oftener than the goat?

The fragment of which these lines are a free version are quoted, it
is true, by Athenaius, Lucian, and Porson from the Myrmidones
and have been placed by Wilkes and Droyssen to the second
tragedy of the Achillean trilogy. I think, if the reader has no objec-
tion, that we can just as well leave them here, altho' Ernest might
certainly have forgotten that they belong to another play of
Aeschylus which he might also have seen during his residence at
Athens.

Song

The snake is come out,
And the bee is about,
In the sunny delight of Hymettus;
O would we were he,
The gay dappled bee,
For then the Narcissus would let us
Drink out of her bosom,
Ambrosian blossom,
To the health of her neighbour, the Olive,
The first drop of spring;
Oh! happy the thing
That in Greece the mellifluous can so live.

The green frog of the ditch,
Pours his love loud and rich,
Coaxing the water-maid's shoulder,
And round golden eyes
Darts in amorous wise
A sheaf of love's bee-stings like arrows;
And Love's in the wood,
In a goat-footed mood,
Dancing with Pan and his fellows;
So the nymphs may take care
Of their treasury rare
Of bosoms and cheeks the sun mellows.

But here oh ho! cold,
Snowy mountainous, old,
Is the earth of the barbarous island.
Through the icicles white
Pale beams the cold light,
Like the life through the coldblooded fish-eye.
[…]

'Before we proceed to the solemnity of the coronation,' said Norman who had now recovered some spirits out of a bottle of Madeira before him (thanks to the adulterators), after offering his congratulations to the conqueror – 'let me sing you a hymn of triumph, in which I defend my own opinions on the subject of this night's discussion. ...'

Who tames the lion now?
Who smoothes Jove's wrinkles now?
Who is the reckless wight
  That in the horrid middle
Of the deserted night
Doth play upon man's brain,
  As on a wanton fiddle,
The mad and magic strain,
The reeling, tripping sound,
To which the world goes round?
  Sing heigh! ho! diddle!
      And then say –
Love, quotha, Love? Nay, nay!
It is a spirit fine
Of ale or ancient wine,
  Lord Alcohol, the drunken fay,
      Lord Alcohol alway!

Who maketh pipe-clay man
Think all that nature can?
Who dares the gods to flout,
  Lay fate beneath the table,
And maketh him stammer out
  A thousand monstrous things,
  For history a fable,
  Dish-clouts for kings?
And sends the world along
Singing a ribald song
  Of heigh-ho! Babel?
      Who, I pray –

Love, quotha, Love? Nay, nay!
It is a spirit fine
Of ale or ancient wine,
  Lord Alcohol, the drunken fay,
      Lord Alcohol alway!

A thousand buds are breaking
    Their prisons silently;
A thousand birds are making
    Their nests in leafy tree;
A thousand babes are waking
    On woman's breast to-day;
    [...]
    Is born to man, to-day
    Beneath the sun of May:
Whence come ye, babes of flowers, and, Children,
    whence come we?

The snow falls by thousands into the sea;
  A thousand blossoms covers
    The forsaken forest,
  And on its branches hovers
    The lark's song thousandfold;
  And maidens hear from lovers
    A thousand secrets guessed
    In June's abundant breast
    Before and yet are blessed –
Whence, blossoms rich, birds bold, beloved maidens,
    whence come ye?

The snow falls by thousands into the sea;
  A thousand flowers are shedding
    Their leaves all dead and dry;
  A thousand birds are threading
    Their passage through the sky;
  A thousand mourners treading
    The tearful churchyard way
    In funeral array:
Birds, whither fly ye? – whither, dead, pass ye?
The snow falls by thousands into the sea.

Other Later Poems & Fragments

Here is something of old Walther von der Vogelweide, who wrote in the earlier part of the 13th century; but in his old German it is infinitely better.

Under the lime tree on the daisied ground
  Two that I know of made their bed.
There you may see heaped and scattered round
  Grass and blossoms broken and shed
    All in a thicket down in the dale;
Tandaradei – sweetly sang the nightingale.
Ere I set foot in the meadow, already
  Some one was waiting for somebody;
There was a meeting – Oh! gracious lady,
  There is no pleasure again for me,
    Thousands of kisses there he took,
Tandaradei – see my lips, how red they look.
Leaf and blossom he had pulled and piled
  For a couch, a green one, soft and high;
And many a one hath gazed and smiled
  Passing the bower and pressed grass by:
    And the roses crushed hath seen,
Tandaradei, where I laid my head between;
  In this love-passage if any one had been there,
How sad and shamed should I be;
  But what were we a doing alone among the green there
No soul shall ever know except my love and me,
    And the little nightingale
  Tandaradei – she, I wot, will tell no tale.

Doomsday

If I can raise one ghost, why I will raise
And call up doomsday from behind the east.
Awake then, ghostly doomsday!
Throw up your monuments, ye buried men
That lie in ruined cities of the wastes!
Ye battle fields, and woody mountain sides,
Ye lakes and oceans, and ye lava floods
That have o'erwhelmed great cities, now roll back!
And let the sceptred break their pyramids,
An earthquake of the buried shake the domes
Of arched cathedrals, and o'erturn the forests,
Until the grassy mounds and sculptured floors,
The monumental statues, hollow rocks,
The paved churchyard, and the flowery mead,
And ocean's billowy sarcophagi,
Pass from the bosoms of the rising
Like clouds! Enough of stars and suns immortal
Have risen in heaven: to-day in earth and sea
Riseth mankind. And first yawn deep
Ye marble palace-floors,
And let the uncoffined bones, which ye conceal,
Ascend, and dig their purple murderers up,
Out of their crowned death. Ye catacombs
Open your gates, and overwhelm the sands
With an eruption of the naked millions,
Out of old centuries! The buried navies
Shall hear the call, and shoot up from the sea
Whose wrecks shall knock against the hollow mountains
And wake the swallowed cities in their hearts.
Forgotten armies rattle with their spears
Against the rocky walls of their sepulchres:
An earthquake of the buried shakes the pillars
Of the thick-sown cathedrals; guilty forests,
Where bloody spades have dug 'mid nightly storms;

The muddy drowning-places of the babes;
The pyramids, and bony hiding-places, –
[…]
'Thou rainbow on the tearful lash of doomsday's morning star
Rise quick, and let me gaze into that planet deep and far,
        As into a loved eye;
Or I must, like the fiery child of the Vesuvian womb,
Burst with my flickering ghost abroad, before the sun of doom
        Rolls up the spectre sky.'

A lowly mound, at stormy night, sent up this ardent prayer
    Out of a murderer's grave, a traitor's nettly bed,
And the deeds of him, more dread than Cain, whose wickedness
                                                        lay there,
    All mankind hath heard or read.
[…]
'What's o'clock?' –
'It wants a quarter to twelve,
And to-morrow's doomsday.'

SONG

'Oh doomsday, doomsday come! thou creative morn
Of graves in earth, and under sea, all teeming at the horn
        Of angels fair and dread.
As thou the ghosts shall waken, so I, the ghost, wake thee;
For thy rising sun and I shall rise together from the sea,
        The eldest of the dead.'

So crying, o'er the billowy main, an old ghost strode
        To a churchyard on the shore,
O'er whose ancient corpse the billowy main of ships had ebbed and
                                                        flowed,
        Four thousand years or more.
    And pale and wan and weary
        Looked never a sprite as he,

For it's lonely and it's dreary
        The ghost of a body to be
That has mouldered long ages away in the sea.
            None has wept upon its stone,
            And ne'er a flower has grown
            Out of its broken heart to prove
How in life it abounded with longings of sweet love.
[…]
'World, wilt thou yield thy spirits up and be convulsed and die?
And as I haunt the billowy main, thy ghost shall haunt the sky,
        A pale unheeded star,
When doomsday, doomsday, doth dawn at length for me.'
So having prayed in moonlight waves, beneath the shipwrecked sea
        In spectral caverns far,
On moonlight o'er the billowy main an old ghost stepped,
        And the waves their satire sung.
For that shade without a body would fain wickedly have wept
        O'er the maid that lay so young
        'Mong weeds and toadstools hoary;
            But bitter 'twas to see
        How he groaned in the moonlight's glory
            In yearnings of desperate agony:
For he could not wring from his eyes in the sea
            One little tear to shed
            In love above the dead,
        But sighing sunk in the waves away
And lies beside the budding sun of blessed doomsday.

        Oh morning star of doomsday –

The Old Ghost

Over the water an old ghost strode
  To a churchyard on the shore,
And over him the waters had flowed
  A thousand years or more,
And pale and wan and weary
  Looked never a sprite as he;
For it's lonely and it's dreary
  The ghost of a body to be
  That has mouldered away in the sea.

Over the billows the old ghost stepped,
  And the winds in mockery sung;
For the bodiless ghost would fain have wept
  Over the maiden that lay so young
'Mong the thistles and toadstools so hoary.
  And he begged of the waves a tear,
But they shook upwards their moonlight glory,
  And the shark looked on with a sneer
  At his yearning desire and agony.

Song by Siegfried

Lady, was it fair of thee
To seem so passing fair to me?
  Not every star to every eye
    Is fair; and why
Art thou another's share?
  Did thine eyes shed brighter glances,
Thine unkissed bosom heave more fair,
  To his than to my fancies?
    But I'll forgive thee still;
    Thou'rt fair without thy will.
    So be: but never know,
    That 'tis the hue of woe.

Lady, was it fair of thee
To be so gentle still to me?
  Not every lip to every eye
    Should let smiles fly.
  Why didst thou never frown,
    To frighten from my pillow
Love's head, round which Hope wove a crown,
  And saw not 'twas of willow?
    But I'll forgive thee still;
    Thou knew'st not smiles could kill.
    Smile on: but never know,
    I die, nor of what woe.

Dream-Pedlary

If there were dreams to sell,
   What would you buy?
Some cost a passing bell;
   Some a light sigh,
That shakes from Life's fresh crown
Only a roseleaf down.
If there were dreams to sell,
Merry and sad to tell,
And the crier rung the bell,
   What would you buy?

A cottage lone and still,
   With bowers nigh,
Shadowy, my woes to still,
   Until I die.
Such pearl from Life's fresh crown
Fain would I shake me down.
Were dreams to have at will,
This would best heal my ill,
   This would I buy.

But there were dreams to sell,
   Ill didst thou buy;
Life is a dream, they tell,
   Waking, to die.
Dreaming a dream to prize,
Is wishing ghosts to rise;
   And, if I had the spell
   To call the buried, well,
      Which one would I?

If there are ghosts to raise,
   What shall I call,
Out of hell's murky haze,

Heaven's blue hall?
Raise my loved longlost boy
To lead me to his joy.
  There are no ghosts to raise;
  Out of death lead no ways;
    Vain is the call.

Know'st thou not ghosts to sue?
  No love thou hast.
Else lie, as I will do,
  And breathe thy last.
So out of Life's fresh crown
Fall like a roseleaf down.
  Thus are the ghosts to woo;
  Thus are all dreams made true,
    Ever to last!

Mandrake. Respect the grave and sober, I pray thee. To-morrow I know thee not. In truth I mark that our noble faculty is in its last leaf. The dry-rot of prudence hath eaten the Ship of Fools to dust; she is no more seaworthy. The fool, who signifies humanity, is laid aside and will soon be forgotten, for why should the feast of asses come but once a year when all the days are foaled of one mother? O world, world, the gods and fairies left you, for thou wert too grave, and now, Socratic star, thy Demon, thy great Pan, Folly, is waning from thy side. The oracles still talked in their sleep, shall our grand-children say, till Master Merryman's Kingdom was broken up; now is every man his own Fool, and Fate for us all. So much for my dying speech and confession as the last Fool, or indeed, the last Man, for he who hath no leaven of the original father Donkey in any corner of him, may be an angel, black, white or piebald: he has lost his title to humanity. And now a ballad to the speech, a rhyme to the reason:

> Folly hath now turned out of door
> Mankind and Fate, who were before
>   Jove's Harlequin and Clown.
> The world's no stage, no tavern more,
>   Its sign the Fool's ta'en down.
> With poppy rain and cypress dew
> Weep all, for all, who laughed for you:
> For goose-grass is no medicine more,
> But the owl's brown eye's the sky's new blue.
>   Heigho! Foolscap!

Mandrake. […] Hear you no noise? Here come disturbers.
Titmouse. 'Tis only a hen-ostrich laying eggs like a tailor.
Mandrake. A tailor! Ignorance, that craft is viviparous.
Titmouse. Are they though? What is goose? And why sit they cross-legged but to hatch. Why, it is written in a Bridgewater Treatise that the genus Tailor, – as man and woman's tailor or man-milliner, tailor military or civil, readymoney tailor, and even he that botcheth in a stall – at a certain age become oviparous, and lay eggs like a codfish, which are good poached, and brought to table with spinache, also, in egg-flip.

> Wee, wee tailor,
> Nobody was paler
>   Than wee, wee tailor;
> And nobody was thinner.
> Hast thou mutton-chops for dinner,
> My small-beer sinner,
> My starveling rat, – but haler, –
>   Wee, wee tailor?
>
> Below his starving garret
> Lived an old witch and a parrot, –
>   Wee, wee tailor, –
> Cross, horrid and uncivil,
> For her grandson was the Devil
> Or a chimney-sweeper evil;
> She was sooty too, but paler, –
>   Wee, wee tailor.
>
> Her sooty hen laid stale eggs,
> And then came with his splay legs
>   Wee, wee tailor,
> And stole them all for dinner.
> Then would old witch begin her

Damnations on the sinner, –
'May the thief lay eggs, – but staler;'
   Wee, wee tailor.

   Wee, wee tailor,
Witch watched him like a jailor.
   Wee, wee tailor
Did all his little luck spill.
Tho' he swallowed many a muck's pill,
Yet his mouth grew like a duck's bill,
Crowed like a hen, – but maler, –
   Wee, wee tailor.

Near him did cursed doom stick,
As he perched upon a broomstick, –
   Wee, wee tailor.
It lightened, rained and thundered,
And all the doctors wondered
When he laid above a hundred
Gallinaceous eggs, – but staler, –
   Wee, wee tailor.

A hundred eggs laid daily;
No marvel he looked palely, –
   Wee, wee tailor.
Witch let folks in to see some
Poach'd tailor's eggs; to please 'em
He must cackle on his besom,
Till Fowl-death did prevail o'er
   Wee, wee tailor.

Song from the Ship

To sea! To sea! the calm is o'er;
　The wanton water leaps in sport,
And rattles down the pebbly shore;
　The dolphin wheels, the sea-cows snort,
And unseen Mermaids' pearly song
Comes bubbling up the weeds among.
　Fling broad the sail, dip deep the oar:
　To sea! To sea! the calm is o'er.

To sea! To sea! our wide-winged bark
　Shall billowy cleave its sunny way,
And with its shadow fleet and dark
　Break the caved Tritons' azure ray,
Like mighty eagle soaring light
O'er antelopes on Alpine height.
　The anchor heaves, the ship swings free,
　The sails swell full. To sea, to sea!

From *Death's Jest-Book* γ Act I Scene iv

Enter Fishermen

1st Fisherman. Away to the water, the moon's cloudy.

2nd Fisherman. Push off quick: there's something like a murder in the air.

1st Fisherman. Will it thunder to-night?

2nd Fisherman. Ay, gaily. 'Twere a right evening to die in.

1st Fisherman. Of the ailing of availing ale: let thy nose die purple on strong beer, and stout be thy porter to paradise. Death shall not catch me in his gin till the swallow comes again.

2nd Fisherman. My wife died on such a night, we had no money to have her buried, and she was sunk into the sea. When the moon looks up at me from the water, I always think of her last look. O that last look! I shall ne'er forget it.

1st Fisherman. Come away: the robbers are at our heels. Off, I say.

[They row off singing.

> As mad sexton's bell, tolling
>   For earth's loveliest daughter
> Night's dumbness breaks rolling
>   Ghostlily:
>   So our boat breaks the water
>   Witchingly.
>
> As her look the dream troubles
>   Of her tearful-eyed lover,
> So our sails in the bubbles
>   Ghostlily
>   Are mirrored, and hover
>   Moonily.

From a Letter to T.F. Kelsall, 15 May 1837

As sudden thunder
  Pierces night,
As magic wonder,
  Wild affright,
Rives asunder
  Mens delight,
Our ghost, our corpse and we
  Cleave The Sea.

As flieth lizard
  Serpent fell,
As goblin grizard
  From the spell
Of pale wizard
  Sinks to hell;
Our life, our laugh, our lay
  Pass away.

As startle morning
  Trumpets bright,
As snowdrop scorning
  Winter's might
Rises warning
  Like a spright:
We buried, dead and slain
  Rise again

From *Death's Jest-Book* γ Act I Scene iv

Song from the Waters

As sudden thunder
  Pierces night;
As magic wonder,
  Mad affright
Rives asunder
  Men's delight:
Our ghost, our corpse and we
   Rise to be.

As flies the lizard
  Serpent fell;
As goblin vizard,
  At the spell
Of pale wizard,
  Sinks to hell;
Our life, our laugh, our lay
   Pass away.

As wake the morning
  Trumpets bright;
As snowdrop, scorning
  Winter's might,
Rises warning
  Like a sprite:
The buried, dead, and slain
   Rise again.

[*Sibylla.*] Dead, is he? What's that further than a word,
Hollow as is the armour of a ghost
Whose chinks the moon he haunts doth penetrate.
Belief in death is the fell superstition,
That hath appalled mankind and chained it down,
A slave unto the dismal mystery
Which old opinion dreams beneath the tombstone.
Dead is he, and the grave shall wrap him up?
And this you see is he? And all is ended?
Aye this is cold, that was a glance of him
Out of the depth of his immortal self;
This utterance and token of his being
His spirit hath let fall, and now is gone
To fill up nature and complete her being.
The form, that here is fallen, was the engine,
Which drew a great motion of spiritual power
Out of the world's own soul, and made it play
In visible motion, as the lofty tower
Leads down the animating fire of heaven
To the world's use. That utensil is broken,
Which did appropriate to human functions
A portion of the ghostly element,
And in another sphere the spirit works:
This then is all your Death. Say not he's dead, –
The word is vile – but that he is henceforth
No more excepted from Eternity.
If he were dead I should indeed despair.
Can a man die? Ay, as the sun doth set:
It is the earth that falls away from light;
Fixed in the heavens, although unseen by us,
The immortal life and light remains triumphant.
And therefore you shall never see me wail,
Or drop base waters of an ebbing sorrow;
No wringing hands, no sighings, no despair,

No mourning weeds will I betake me to;
But keep my thought of him that is no more,
As secret as great nature keeps his soul,
From all the world; and consecrate my being
To that divinest hope, which none can know of
Who have not laid their dearest in the grave.

Dirge

Sorrow, lie still and wear
No tears, no sighings, no despair,
No trembling dewy smile of care,
    No mourning weeds,
  Nought that discloses
    A heart that bleeds;
But looks contented I will bear,
  And o'er my cheeks strew roses.
Unto the world I may not weep,
But save my sorrow all, and keep
  A secret heart, sweet soul, for thee,
    As the great earth and swelling sea —

Song

In lover's ear a wild voice cried:
   'Sleeper, awake and rise!'
A pale form stood by his bed-side,
   With heavy tears in her sad eyes.
'A beckoning hand, a moaning sound,
A new-dug grave in weedy ground
For her who sleeps in dreams of thee.
Awake! Let not the murder be!'
Unheard the faithful dream did pray,
And sadly sighed itself away.
   'Sleep on,' sung Sleep, 'to-morrow
   'Tis time to know thy sorrow.'
   'Sleep on,' sung Death, 'to-morrow
   From me thy sleep thou'lt borrow.'
   Sleep on, lover, sleep on,
   The tedious dream is gone;
      The bell tolls one.

Another hour, another dream:
   'Awake! awake!' it wailed,
'Arise, ere with the moon's last beam
   Her rosy life hath paled.
A hidden light, a muffled tread,
A daggered hand beside the bed
Of her who sleeps and dreams of thee.
Thou wak'st not: let the murder be.'
In vain the faithful dream did pray,
And sadly sighed itself away.
   'Sleep on,' sung Sleep, 'to-morrow
   'Tis time to know thy sorrow.'
   'Sleep on,' sung Death, 'to-morrow
   From me thy sleep thou'lt borrow.'

Sleep on, lover, sleep on,
The tedious dream is gone;
    Soon comes the sun.

Another hour, another dream:
  A red wound on a snowy breast,
A rude hand stifling the last scream,
  On rosy lips a death-kiss pressed.
Blood on the sheets, blood on the floor,
The murderer stealing through the door.
'Now,' said the voice, with comfort deep,
'She sleeps indeed, and thou may'st sleep.'
The scornful dream then turned away
To the first, weeping cloud of day.
  'Sleep on,' sung Sleep, 'to-morrow
  'Tis time to know thy sorrow.'
  'Sleep on,' sung Death, 'to-morrow
  From me thy sleep thou'lt borrow.'
  Sleep on, lover, sleep on,
  The tedious dream is gone;
    The murder's done.

Song from the Waters

The swallow leaves her nest,
The soul my weary breast;
But therefore let the rain
 On my grave
Fall pure; for why complain?
Since both will come again
 O'er the wave.

The wind dead leaves and snow
Doth hurry to and fro;
And, once, a day shall break
 O'er the wave,
When a storm of ghosts shall shake
The dead, until they wake
 In the grave.

Draft of *Death's Jest-Book* γ III.i.40ff.

I followed once a fleet and mighty serpent
Into a cavern in a mountain's side;
And, wading many lakes, descending gulphs,
At last I reached the ruins of a city,
Built not like ours but of another world,
As if the aged earth had loved in youth
The mightiest city of a perished planet,
And kept the image of it in her heart,
So dream-like, shadowy, and spectral was it.
Nought seemed alive there, and the very dead
Were of another world the skeletons.
The mammoth, ribbed like to an arched cathedral,
Lay there, and ruins of great creatures else
More like a shipwrecked fleet, too great they seemed
For all the life that is to animate:
And vegetable rocks, tall sculptured palms,
Pines grown, not hewn, in stone; and giant ferns,
Whose earthquake-shaken leaves bore graves for nests.

Away, away, thou soarest, happy bird,
With pealing song and hearty clap of wings,
Cheerily rowing through the sea of air
Thy little boat of life high overhead,
Startling the gaze of lofty capricorns
On mountain pinnacle; now glidest thou
Softly to settle on a flowering spray
Gay as May morning, love-thought on the eyelid
Of simple maiden; thence to dart ere long
Full of heedless song and caring nought
For the tear shed at parting: When thy day,
Spent so in sunshine, darkens, thou art welcomed
In the warm bosom of thy feathery home
By patient mate; and I must hear thee toying
Until the very thought of liberty
Is in my dreams, a bird whose nest is built –

Far away,
　　As we hear
The song of wild swans winging
　　Through the day,
The thought of him, who is no more, comes ringing
　　On my ear.

　　Gentle fear
　　On the breast
Of my memory comes breaking,
　　Near and near,
As night winds' murmurous music waking
　　Seas at rest.

　　As the blest
　　Tearful eye
Sees the sun behind the ocean
　　Red i' th' west,
Grow pale, and in changing hues and fading motion
　　Wane and die:

　　So do I
　　Wake or dream

Crowned with icy gold
And laurel, dew[ed] with blood,
Up among pale slaves stood
Tiberius

*   *   *

Tiberius Caesar, robed in blood,
Palest among pale Romans, stood
That highest height
Of Alp i' the sun's last gush of light,
Around whose rocky

Dim shone the pallid torches' trembling ray
And the last gush of voices died away,
As bleeds the sunshine of a stormswept day
        Upon a panting sea.
[…]
A cloudlike ruin, tempest-overcast,
Lay bursting hearts, and listened for the blast
Of trumpet, the dead-awakening, last,
        'Mid wailing of
      Miserere mei domine.

The hearts were heaped, and through them lightning passed
The thought of the last trump's dead-kindling blast;
Then met the prostrate wretches' tearful gaze,
Moved with the waving incense' circling haze,
The Sistine wall with Michael's wrath ablaze:
        The Judge of mercy weary,
        The Demon's vengeful glee.

The rainbow-prism of heaven's choired daughters,
Wafted athwart downdashed entwined slaughters
Of countless damned – So break and fall, waters,
        With miserere
      Into Eternity.

Who lonely strays in England's oaky forest
    Meets silence drear the windless leaves among
Since thou no more Æolian breathings pourest
  O'er Ocean's crowned isle, Spirit of Song.
Silence unknown to Druid-spectre hoarest
    Since Merlin bid thy disenchanted tongue
  Above the nations, as a bird on high
  O'er Alpine tops, arouse
  A cataractous burst of ceaseless melody.

Where are the masters of the magic word,
    Who reallumed the Promethean blaze
And let old Ocean out with all his herd
    On the Atlantic sufferer's front to gaze?
Where he, whose satire sharper than sharp sword
    Flashed and fell deep, unparried by amaze?
  Where he, of heath and lake most loved of all
  In lady's bower and castled tower and hall
  With fairy-footed, dancing thoughts and longings musical?

Though few might weep when the Ægean rose,
    Deaf and tumultuous as human kind,
To overwhelm for ever in its close
    The purest summits of an Alpine mind,
Shelley has sweet revenge: him crowning grows
  Spite of the bigots and their patent moral,
  Above the region of eternal quarrel
  […]
  In all their lightnings' spite, luxurious laurel.

And he of lofty brow and pen of iron,
    Old Goethe's darling, where the night is Grecian
In some Elysium pets his Houri-syren
    Or jokes with Rabelais, the head's physician,
About the sour archbooby who shut Byron
    Out of the Abbey –

What silence drear in England's oaky forest,
Erst merry with the redbreast's ballad song
Or rustic roundelay! No hoof-print on the sward,
Where sometime danced Spenser's equestrian verse
Its mazy measure! Now by pathless brook
Gazeth alone the broken-hearted stag,
And sees no tear fall in from pitiful eye
Like kindest Shakespeare's. We, who marked how fell
Young Adonais, sick of vain endeavour
Larklike to live on high in tower of song;
And looked still deeper thro' each other's eyes
At every flash of Shelley's dazzling spirit,
Quivering like dagger on the breast of night,
That seemed some hidden natural light reflected
Upon time's scythe, a moment and away:
Darkness unfathomable over it.
We, who have seen Mount Rydal's snowy head
Bound round with courtly jingles; list so long
Like old Orion for the break of morn,
Like Homer blind for sound of youthful harp;
And, if a wandering music swells the gale,
'Tis some poor solitary heartstring burst.
Well, Britain; let the fiery Frenchman boast
That at the bidding of the charmer moves
Their nation's heart, as ocean 'neath the moon
Silvered and soothed. Be proud of Manchester,
Pestiferous Liverpool, Ocean-Avernus,
Where bullying blasphemy, like a slimy lie,
Creeps to the highest church's pinnacle,
And glistening infects the light of heaven.
O flattering likeness on a copper coin!
Sit still upon your slave-raised cotton ball,
With upright toasting fork and toothless cat:
The country clown still holds her for a lion.
The voice, the voice! when the affrighted herds
Dash heedless to the edge of craggy abysses,
And the amazed circle of scared eagles

Spire to the clouds, amid the gletscher clash
When avalanches fall, nation-alarums –
But clearer, though not loud, a voice is heard
Of proclamation or of warning stern.
   Yet, if I tread out of the Alpine shade,
And once more weave the web of thoughtful verse,
May no vainglorious motive break my silence;
If I have sate unheard so long, it was in hope
That mightier and better might assay
The potent spell to break, which has fair Truth
Banished so drear a while from mouths of song.
Though genius, bearing out of other worlds
New freights of thought from fresh-discovered mines,
Be but reciprocated love of Truth:
Witness kind Shakespeare, our recording angel,
Newton, whose thought rebuilt the universe,
And Galileo, broken-hearted seer,
Who, like a moon attracted naturally,
Kept circling round the central sun of Truth.
Not in the popular playhouse, or full throng
Of opera-gazers longing for deceit;
Not on the velvet day-bed, novel-strewn,
Or in the interval of pot and pipe;
Not between sermon and the scandalous paper,
May verse like this e'er hope an eye to feed on't.
But if there be, who, having laid the loved
Where they may drop a tear in roses' cups,
With half their hearts inhabit other worlds;
If there be any – ah! were there but few –
Who watching the slow lighting up of stars,
Lonely at eve, like seamen sailing near
Some island city where their dearest dwell,
Cannot but guess in sweet imagining –
Alas! too sweet, doubtful, and melancholy –
Which light is glittering from their loved one's home:
Such may perchance, with favourable mind,
Follow my thought along its mountainous path.

Now then to Caucasus, the cavernous. –
[...]

*   *   *

Does any lip of lady drop, like dew,
Upon the sleeping youngling's pearly cheek?
What silence ghastly.

*   *   *

Yet who hath looked into the eye of truth
And seen mankind after the will of nature,
Should live the fair and innocent life of flowers.

I have looked at your letter again and am *not* convinced by it that it is my business to get anything printed. 20 years ago I was so over-rated, that of course I must fall short of all reasonable and unreasonable expectation. Times are much changed, it is true. I am not aware that there's one single fellow, who has the least nose for poetry, that writes. You seem to take Tea-leaves for Bay: which is all very natural and Chinese, according to the national Anthem,

Drink, Britannia, Britannia drink your Tea,
For Britons, Bores and butter'd Toast; they all begins with B.

Through robe and rib and muscle to heart's core
We see as stars through clear midnight.

The Phantom-Wooer

A ghost, that loved a lady fair,
Ever in the starry air
   Of midnight at her pillow stood;
And, with a sweetness skies above
The luring words of human love,
   Her soul the phantom wooed.
Sweet and sweet is their poisoned note,
The little snakes of silver throat,
In mossy skulls that nest and lie,
Ever singing 'die, oh! die.'

Young soul put off your flesh, and come
With me into the quiet tomb,
   Our bed is lovely, dark, and sweet;
The earth will swing us, as she goes,
Beneath our coverlid of snows,
   And the warm leaden sheet.
Dear and dear is their poisoned note,
The little snakes of silver throat,
In mossy skulls that nest and lie,
Ever singing 'die, oh! die.'

I am bewildered – utterly astray
Within the doubt-brakes of obscurest Thought,
Whereunto at the last I have been brought
Thro' all diversity of time & way
Not blindfold, unaware [& in dismay
Up from my used haunts suddenly caught
By some strange Doubt, pledgling of Chance & –]

Who walks upon the dew with step less loud,
Than the fed wind quitting the full blown rose,
Whose flusht leaves scorn to waver as he goes?

*   *   *

He lies upon the earth, beneath the sun,
Rankling the air, –
[...]
        beyond all virtue less profound
Than love

*   *   *

Pleased with the gratitude of nobler men

Far happier am I here, being alone,
Than if my heart were emptied, in a croud,
Of its own passion, to be filled anew
With unknown mixtures even of the best –
Or left to air – yet is there now not far
A company of mortal sympathies
Wherein I would be –

*   *   *

For ever wandering, yet ne'er astray –

Harcourt Bdgs., Temple, London
[*Postmark* May 29, 1847]

My dear Kelsall,

The author of all those celebrated unwritten productions, amongst which I particularly solicit your attention to a volume of letters to yourself, will leave the station for Fareham at seven o'clock to-morrow, and stay Sunday at that place:

> Poor bird, that cannot ever
> Dwell high in tower of song:
> Whose heart-breaking endeavour
> But palls the lazy throng!

T. L. B.

Notes

References

Bradshaw, Michael. *Resurrection Songs: The Poetry of Thomas Lovell Beddoes* (Aldershot and Burlington: Ashgate, 2001)

Death's Jest-Book, β. The earlier version; the most recent edition is *Death's Jest-Book: The 1829 text*, ed. Michael Bradshaw (Manchester and New York: Carcanet/Routledge, 2003)

Death's Jest-Book, γ. The later version: see 'West House' below.

Donner, *Works. The Works of Thomas Lovell Beddoes*, ed. with an introduction by H.W. Donner (London: Oxford University Press, 1935)

Gosse. *The Poetical Works of Thomas Lovell Beddoes*, ed. with a memoir by Edmund Gosse (London: Dent, 1890)

Kelsall. *The Poems Posthumous and Collected of Thomas Lovell Beddoes, with a Memoir*, ed. T.F. Kelsall, 2 vols. (London: William Pickering, 1851)

West House. *Death's Jest-Book; or, The Day will Come*, ed. Alan Halsey (Sheffield: West House, 2003)

17. 'Chapter I.' Donner records two cancelled lines which were probably the beginning of an epigraph:

> Four friends under the rose
> When in the bud ruffled by Sir W. Davenant's nose

17. 'Shall I be your first love ...' Kelsall's title: 'Love-in-Idleness'.

18. 'Lament of Thanatos'. The title appears to be Donner's, retained in brackets since it justifies the placement.

19. 'Thanatos to Kenelm.' Dykes Campbell note, *Works* p.700. A female Thanatos seems to be one of Beddoes' idiosyncrasies.

20. 'Epilogue to Chapter I.' Kelsall's title: 'Dial-Thoughts'.

22. 'Chapter II.' 'The Lily Plucked by Proserpine: cancelled title 'The Passion Flower and the Lily'. The second epigraph is a variant of *Death's Jest-Book* V.iv.236-8:

I wondered how so fair a thing could live:
And, now she is no more, it seems to me
She was too beautiful ever to die!

22. 'The Tale of the Lover ...' Published in *The Examiner*, 8 October 1864 under the title 'Cupid, Death, and Psyche. An Apologue by the Late Thomas Lovell Beddoes'. The title is presumably due to Kelsall, who contributes an introductory note: 'The piece, now published, belongs to "The Lily Plucked by Proserpine", one of the prose-tales designed by their author to form part of his unfinished "Ivory Gate", and has therein a special appositeness, being the narration of a lover to his mistress, in the sportive exuberance of delight, on the eve of their intended marriage – in reality of her seizure and trial, condemnation and execution, on a wrongful charge of murder. The tale itself – a "pansy freak'd with jet" – in its unfolding of beauty and happiness – its fresh joy-blossoms so ruthlessly and mysteriously crushed – and its haunting images of tenderness and affection, is prefigured, with a quaint and delicate fidelity, in the lines which were written by the author as a motto to it: [quotes "In the twilight silent smiled"].'

23. 'Epilogue to Human Woe.' Kelsall's title: 'The Ballad of Human Life'.

26. 'O Lie ...' In fact a variant of *Death's Jest-Book* γ I.i.283-9:

O Lie, O Lie, O lovely lady Lie,
They told me that thou art the devil's daughter.
Then thou art greater than thy father, Lie;
For while he mopes in Hell, thou queen'st it bravely,
Ruling the earth under the name of Truth,
While she is at the bottom of the well,
Where Joseph left her.

27. 'The New Cecilia.' Text from Beddoes' letter to Kelsall, 15 May 1837 (*Works* pp.661-7). The preceding passage reads: 'My fingers are now so cold that I must put them into my pockets and sing you a very objectionable piece of foolery, enough to ruin the reputation of any one, who wishes to introduce his writings into good society. – Allons! It's a sparkling piece of anecdote, filed out of the golden Legend, and extracted from Chap V of the Ivory Gate – or lesser Dionysiacs – (my new book –)'. In the γ text of *Death's Jest-Book* a slightly revised version in regular stanzas is sung by Mandrake: for variants cf. *Death's Jest-Book* γ I.iv.19-48. The anonymous *Vita* of St Gengulphus was probably written in the 9th

or 10th century and thus predates the *Legenda Aurea*. The name 'Gengul-phus' has a number of German and French variants and it seems likely that Beddoes knew the town of Saint-Gingolph on the south bank of Lake Geneva. In another version of the legend the saint's name appears as 'Gangolf' and the lady is only speechless but flatulent on Fridays. It seems more than coincidental that R.H. Barham's 'Lay of St Gengulphus' was published in the spring 1837 issue of *Bentley's Miscellany*: is Beddoes' poem a riposte? Barham has it that a cushion stuffed with St Gengulphus' beard miraculously and permanently attached itself to his adulterous wife's nether end. Beddoes would have considered this variation much too polite although as Christine Hankinson has pointed out Barham's conclusion may have amused him: 'So this shocking bad wife heard a voice all her life / Crying "Murder!" resound from the cushion – or thereabouts.'

29. 'Has no one seen my heart of you?' Donner prints this poem twice, as the motto to 'Chapter Last' and among the unplaced poems and frag-ments (*Works* pp.121 & 125). Kelsall's title: 'The Runaway'.

33. 'As I passed over the bridge …' Kelsall's title: 'Alpine Spirit's Song'. Donner's note: "'See Hegetschweiler, p.44." The reference is to his friend Johannes Hegetschweiler's *Reisen in dem Gebirgstock zwischen Glarus und Graubünden in den Jahren 1819, 1820 und 1822*, Zürich, 1825, pp.41-5: *Beschreibung der Gletscher der Sandalp*. Dykes Campbell transcribes 'p.77', but this must be a scribal error for '44'. The Sandalp is situated at the foot of the Tödi when approached from the north through Linthal.' (*Works* p.700) The poem may contain other allusions to Hegetschweiler's botanical stud-ies of the Tödi and its environs; gentians were one of his particular inter-ests. 'Pilate' refers to the mountain near Lucerne where Pontius Pilate is said to have drowned in a tarn; one of his ghostly manifestations is as a cave-dwelling dragon.

35. 'The Reason Why'. The poem also appears in *Death's Jest-Book* γ I.iii.62-97 where it is sung by one of Wolfram's knights.

37. 'The Tree of Life.' Donner includes this fragment in *The Ivory Gate* on grounds of 'theme and sentiment'. 'Kelsall is the sole authority, and we know neither when it was written nor where the manuscript was to be found. Its familiarity with Scandinavian mythology establishes undeniable evidence that it was written after Beddoes had left England' (*Works* p.xxxvii).

38. 'The Bells rang out …' Kelsall's title: 'Dirge and Hymeneal'. The fragment apparently relates to the marriage/death theme of Chapter II but it also suggests an unrealised development of *Death's Jest-Book*. 'Sibald' (sic) appears as a son of Duke Melveric among the 'Persons Represented' on the draft title page of the γ text of *Death's Jest-Book* although the son who is eventually murdered is, as in the β text, called Athulf throughout.

40. 'At break of bright May morning.' Kelsall's title: 'The Two Archers'.

42. 'The Lily of the Valley.' Dykes Campbell records that this poem was transcribed 'from a very imperfect scrap' (*Works* p.xxxvii).

45. 'What do you think the mermaids …' Donner retains the title 'Song of the Stygian Naiades' which he says 'seems to be Kelsall's'. In the MS the poem was written on the same sheet as 'Dirge' (*Works* p.xxxvii).

48. 'And in that rosy rosy hour'. Donner's title: 'The Rosy Hour'.

50. 'Flowed many a woodbird's voice …'. Donner's title: 'The City of the Sea'. In the MS this fragment was written on the same scrap as 'The Flowery Alchymist' (*Works* p.xxxvii).

51. 'Silenus in Proteus.' Donner's note: 'Among the seventy-three plays of Aeschylus, mentioned in the text appended to the seven plays in the eleventh-century Codex Mediceus or Laurentianus, are the *Myrmidons* and the *Proteus*. The former, together with the *Nereids* and the *Phrygians*, formed a trilogy supposedly dealing with episodes in the life of Achilles. The *Proteus*, according to the 'Argumentum ad Agamemnona' in the Codex Mediceus, was the satyric drama acted after the *Oresteia* on its first public presentation. The lines that survive bear no resemblance to *Silenus in Proteus.*' (*Works* p.700)

52. 'Song.' In the MS this fragment was written on the same sheet as 'Silenus in Proteus' (*Works* p.xxxvii).

53. 'Before we proceed …' Gosse's title: 'Lord Alcohol'.

59. 'Here is something …' Introduction and text from letter to Kelsall, April 1829 (*Works* p.646). *Works* p.98 divides the poem into four stanzas, regularising the layout and punctuation.

60. 'Doomsday.' The usual reading of line 16 is 'Pass from the bosoms of the rising people', although Donner notes that in the MS 'people' was 'erased and nothing substituted' (*Works* p.106, footnote). I have followed Michael Bradshaw's suggestion that 'it is quite possible that no other word was intended […] Beddoes could be seen to have coined a noun for a category of people in between death and afterlife that might correspond with "the living" and "the dead", or even with categories such as "the saved", "the damned", and "the elect". The implication would be that the condition of rising, of being in violent transition between states, constitutes a distinct order of being. In addition to this primary meaning of "rising", a reader might also be aware of "rising" in the sense of "rebellion".' (*Resurrection Songs* p.193)

63. 'The Old Ghost.' First published in Gosse's edition. Donner comments that the poem 'presents no small difficulty. Gosse is here the sole textual authority, and it would not be impossible to extract his version from the rough draft of the song at the end of *Doomsday*. But in July 1830 Beddoes told Kelsall that he had sent Bourne a Song "about an old ghost", and it is not unlikely that a clean copy had found its way into the Browning box and was published by Gosse. Whether it had been removed later, or simply overlooked by Dykes Campbell, who is to say?' (*Works* p.xxxv.)

64. 'Song by Siegfried.' *Death's Jest-Book* γ IV.iii.194-217.

67. 'From *Death's Jest-Book* γ Act I Scene i.' Lines 45-70 in *Works*; 43-73 in West House. The poem is titled 'Fragment' by Gosse, 'Mandrake's Song' by Donner.

68. 'From *Death's Jest-Book* γ Act I Scene iv.' Lines 64-121 in *Works*; 65-123 in West House. The poem was first published by Gosse under the title 'The Oviparous Tailor'.

70. 'Song from the Ship.' *Death's Jest-Book* γ I.i.290-305 (*Works*; 299-314 in West House), with slightly variant punctuation.

71. 'From *Death's Jest-Book* γ Act I Scene iv.' Lines 122-147 in *Works*; 124-149 in West House. The poem was printed separately by Kelsall as 'Song on the Water'. The passage is an example of the increasingly random nature of the later additions to *Death's Jest-Book*. The fishermen are introduced solely to sing the song, which has no dramatic relevance. Titmouse

is similarly introduced to sing 'Wee, wee tailor'; his song is also dramatically extraneous although as a fine example of fool's nonsense it is at least in character. It seems less likely that these fishermen would sing so exquisite a shanty. Mandrake's 'Folly hath now turned out of door' is on the other hand entirely integrated.

72-3. 'From a Letter to T.F. Kelsall, 15 May 1837' & 'From *Death's Jest-Book* γ Act I Scene iv' (lines 204-227 in *Works*; 206-229 in West House). Both versions are included because their relatively slight variations affect the nuance and flow of this highly-wrought poem. For its separate appearance in *Works* pp.115-6, where 'Wild' is retained instead of 'Mad' in line 4, Donner gives the title 'The Warning', a reference to the preceding lines

> [*Duke.*] Let my name burn through all dark history
> Over the waves of time, as from a lighthouse,
> Warning approach.
> *Wolfram.* I will avenge me, Duke, as never man.

In earlier editions of *Death's Jest-Book* the poem appears at the end of IV.ii under the heading '*Voices in the air*', following Sibylla's speech ending

> O Death! I am thy friend,
> I struggle not with thee. I love thy state:
> Thou canst be sweet and gentle, be so now;
> And let me pass praying away into thee,
> As twilight still does into starry night.

74. 'Draft of *Death's Jest-Book* γ II.ii.36ff.' Donner suggests that this passage was written at Würzburg in 1831 or 1832, to be replaced by the 'final' γ version a few years later (*Works* p.xliii). The *Dirge* as printed here combines two variants; in one the first line is omitted and the other omits the third.

76. 'From *Death's Jest-Book* γ Act I Scene iii.' Kelsall's title: 'The Boding Dreams'. The song first appears in a letter, 13 November 1844, with the comment 'I have stuck it into the endless J.B.' (*Works* p.674) 'Stuck it in' accurately reflects its lack of dramatic relevance. It appears at the opening of the scene, where Sibylla, Wolfram and knights are found in a 'Tent on the Sea-shore'. The unidentified singer must be one of the knights, for when the song has ended Wolfram comments

> Sing me no more such ditties: they are well
> For the last gossips, when the snowy wind
> Howls in the chimney till the very taper
> Trembles with its blue flame, and the bolted gates
> Rattle before old winter's palsied hand.
> If you will sing, let it be cheerily
> Of dallying love. There's many a one among you
> Hath sung, beneath our oak trees to his maiden,
> Light bird-like mockeries, fit for love in springtime.
> Sing such a one.

The same or another knight then sings 'I love thee and I love thee not', which Beddoes had already assigned to *The Ivory Gate*. The songs replace an exchange in blank verse between Wolfram and Sibylla in the β version.

78. 'From *Death's Jest-Book* γ Act I Scene iv.' Lines 259-272 in *Works*; 261-274 in West House. Donner's title 'Wolfram's Dirge'. The song first appears in the same letter as 'In lover's ear'. It closes Act I, in response to Wolfram's death, replacing a blank verse exchange between the Duke, Sibylla and a knight in the β version. It has dramatic relevance in that it foreshadows Wolfram's resurrection in Act III.

79. 'Draft of *Death's Jest-Book* γ III.i.40ff.' Beddoes appears to have envisaged this passage as a replacement for, or preface to, the Duke's description of the necromancer Ziba. Its references to the prehistoric world show some affinity with the 'Thanatos to Kenelm' passage in *The Ivory Gate*.

80. 'Draft of *Death's Jest-Book* γ I.ii.84ff.' The passage seems to have been intended as a development of the Duke's paean to Liberty.

81. 'Far away.' Kelsall's title: 'Threnody'.

82. 'Crowned with icy gold.' Donner's title: 'Tiberius Caesar. *Two fragments*'.

83. 'Dim shone the …' Donner's title: 'The Last Judgment'. He records that the text 'had once been a fair copy on [a] scrap, "but", says Dykes Campbell, "pulled to pieces by a later pen – and left bleeding".' (*Works* p.xl)

84. 'Who lonely strays …' Donner proposes 1843 as date of composition and gives the title 'Stanzas Written in Switzerland'. 'The stanzas were

drafted on a loose scrap of paper, and Dykes Campbell tells us that there was "yet another draft in rhyme on the subject – but it is grotesque, and very poor in its grotesquerie of rhyme", and he did not transcribe it.' (*Works* p.xl)

85. 'What silence drear ...' Donner's title: 'Lines Written in Switzerland'. His dating to 1844 is based on the allusion to Wordsworth's appointment as Laureate. He prints the two three-line fragments separately under the title 'Fragments of the Same'.

88. 'I have looked ...' From the letter to Kelsall, 13 November 1844 (*Works* pp.676-7). Donner prints the two verses separately as 'Epigram'.

89. 'Through robe and rib ...' Donner's title: 'Reflexion'. The lines appear in the Dykes Campbell transcript, untitled.

91. 'I am bewildered ...' This fragment appears on a single leaf of MS together with 'Who walks ...', 'He lies ...', 'Pleased ...', 'Far happier ...' and 'For ever ...'; Donner gathers all these under the title 'Last Fragments'. He records that the MS remained with the Kelsall family until it was sold to C.H. Wilkinson in 1930. The square brackets indicate text 'traced in ink over pencilling by a different hand.' (*Works* p.789)

94. 'Harcourt Bdgs. ...' The letter (*Works* p.679) was written during Beddoes' last visit to England. Donner gives the four-line poem the title 'On Himself'.

Index of Titles and First Lines

Titles are given with quotation marks, first lines without. Titles supplied by previous editors are included in italics for cross-reference.

A ghost, that loved a lady fair 90
'Alpine Spirit's Song' 33
And in that rosy rosy hour 48
As mad sexton's bell, tolling 71
As sudden thunder 72
As sudden thunder [*Death's Jest-Book* version] 73
As veined petal closes over 47
At break of bright May morning 40
A thousand buds are breaking...55
Away, away, thou soarest, happy bird 80

Crowned with icy gold...82

Dead, is he? What's that further than a word 74
'Dial-Thoughts' 20
Dim shone the pallid torches' trembling ray...83
'Dirge'...44
'Dirge and Hymeneal'...38
'Doomsday' 60
'Draft of *Death's Jest-Book* γ I.ii.84ff.' 80
'Draft of *Death's Jest-Book* γ II.ii.36ff.'..74
'Draft of *Death's Jest-Book* γ III.i.40ff.' 79
'Dream-Pedlary'..65
Drink, Britannia, Britannia drink your Tea...88

'Epigram' 88
'Epilogue to Chapter I'..20
'Epilogue to Ernest's Story' 29
'Epilogue to Human Woe by Kenelm'..23

Far away 81
Far happier am I here, being alone 93
Flowed many a woodbird's voice, and insects played 50

Folly hath now turned out of door 67
'Fragment' 67
'From a Letter to T.F. Kelsall, 15 May 1837' 72
'From *Death's Jest-Book* γ Act I Scene i' 67
'From *Death's Jest-Book* γ Act I Scene iii' 76
'From *Death's Jest-Book* γ Act I Scene iv' 68
'From *Death's Jest-Book* γ Act I Scene iv' 71
'From *Death's Jest-Book* γ Act I Scene iv' 72
'From *Death's Jest-Book* γ Act I Scene iv' 78

Has no one seen my heart of you...29
He: Shall I be your first love, lady, shall I be your first...............................17
Hist, oh hist...49

I am bewildered – utterly astray 91
If I can raise one ghost, why I will raise...60
I followed once a fleet and mighty serpent...79
If there were dreams to sell...65
I love thee and I love thee not...35
In lover's ear a wild voice cried 76
I think of thee at daybreak still 20
I was to wait, to wait my only time of youth away.......................................18

Lady, was it fair of thee 64
'[Lament of Thanatos]' 18
'Last Fragments' 91-3
Let dew the flowers fill..44
'Lines Written in Switzerland' 85
'Lord Alcohol' 53
'Love-in-Idleness' 17

'Mandrake's Song' 67

O'er the snow, through the air, to the mountain 33
Oh those were happy days, heaped up with wine-skins...............................51
'On Himself' 94
Over the water an old ghost strode 63

Poor bird, that cannot ever...94
Proserpine may pull her flowers 45

'Reflexion' 89

'Silenus in Proteus' 51
'Song' 52
'Song by Siegfried' 64
'Song from the Ship' 70
'Song of the Stygian Naiades' 45
'Song on the Water' 71
'Stanzas Written in Switzerland' 84

'Thanatos to Kenelm' 19
'The Ballad of Human Life' 23
'The Boding Dreams' 76
'The City of the Sea' 50
'The Father of the Deep' 20
'The Flowery Alchymist' 49
'The Last Judgment' 83
'The Lily of the Valley' 42
The mighty thoughts of an old world..19
'The New Cecilia' 27
'The Old Ghost' 63
'The Oviparous Tailor' 68
'The Phantom-Wooer' 90
'The Reason Why' 35
There is a mighty, magic tree 37
'The Rosy Hour' 48
The snake is come out 52
The swallow leaves her nest 78
'[The Tale of the Lover to his Mistress]' 22
'The Tree of Life' 37
'The Two Archers' 40
'The Warning' 73
'Threnody' 81
Through robe and rib and muscle to heart's core 89
'Tiberius Caesar' 82
To sea! To sea! the calm is o'er..70

Under the lime tree on the daisied ground...59

Wee, wee tailor 68
What silence drear in England's oaky forest 85

When we were boy and girl together..23
Where the hare-bells are ringing...42
Whoever has heard of St Gingo...27
Who lonely strays in England's oaky forest..84
Who passed by sea or land...20
Who tames the lion now...53
Who walks upon the dew with step less loud...92
Woe! woe! this is death's hour...38
'Wolfram's Dirge'...78

Also published by ReScript Books...

Dracula's Precursors:
The Mysterious Stranger
& other stories

An evocative setting in the Carpathian Mountains; an enigmatic aristocrat
living alone in a vast ruin who seems to have dominion over wolves; a
vampire who retreats to a coffin in a ruined crypt during the daytime and
can only be vanquished by staking; a beautiful young woman in peril....
No, this isn't *Dracula*, but a story written some 70 years before Bram
Stoker appropriated these elements for his classic novel.

"The Mysterious Stranger" was published anonymously in German in
1823 and translated into English soon after, during a time of enthusiasm
for all things Gothic and Romantic.

Long out of print, it is presented here along with two other less familiar
early vampire tales: **"The Last Lords of Gardonal"** (1867) by William
Gilbert, the father of the famous D'Oyly Carte librettist, and Mary
Cholmondeley's 1890 chiller, **"Let Loose"**.

David Annwn's informative introduction sets the context.

ReScript Books, 2011, ISBN 978-1-874400-49-3, UK price £9.00